Prayers of My Youth

Also by F.S. Yousaf

Euphoria
Sincerely
Serenity
Oaths

Prayers of My Youth

poems

F.S. YOUSAF

Andrews McMeel Publishing
a division of Andrews McMeel Universal
1130 Walnut Street, Kansas City, Missouri 64106

www.andrewsmcmeel.com

24 25 26 27 28 VEP 10 9 8 7 6 5 4 3 2 1

ISBN: 978-1-5248-9433-7

Library of Congress Control Number: 2024937595

Editor: Patty Rice
Art Director/Designer: Julie Barnes
Production Editor: Jennifer Straub
Production Manager: Alex Alfano

To Yusra

For staying through the most turbulent of chapters.

chapters

I – ABLUTION

A clean body, a clean mind, and a clean soul.
What else does a person desire?

My father first taught me how to make *Wudu* (ablution). The way one washes their hands, between each finger and every toe. Water gliding down my wrists and droplets resting in my hair. He would say it was a clean slate–that with every droplet that traveled down my skin, a sin would be entrapped in it. That not only did you cleanse your outward body, but your soul as well. I looked forward to being reborn every time I made *Wudu*.

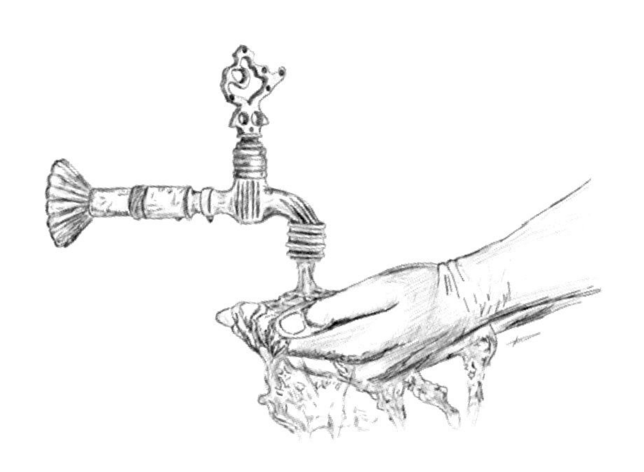

MATURATION

Even though we had departed,

I could never bring myself to wish bad upon you.
I would pray endlessly,
no matter how many pins and needles
would puncture my skin—
no matter how many tears would leave burns on my body.

Because even though it was all I could do,
it would give me peace knowing
some good had happened to you.

THE KITES OF CHILDHOOD (ADOLESCENCE)

My father used to bring home kites
from Pakistan, made out of colorful paper
and thin sticks.

Mine was pink and blue
and caught my eye as soon
as it was taken out. It was beautiful,
and I imagined it soaring through
the skies, viewable from all the houses in town.

The yarn was gray
and had minuscule shards of glass
woven within it.
My father told me that it was for kite fighting,
the way they used to do it from the rooftops
of the villages.

One would fly the kite
and the other would be in charge of the spool.
Together, they would change altitudes
and attempt to cut others' kite strings.
The last kite left in the air would be the winner.

And my mind would run to those rooftops,
the very sand-ridden parapets he had described.
Imagining controlling the kite
with a friend handling the spool behind me.
Together winning the kite-fighter crown,
and my father being proud of his only son.

All while I lay in bed, with a grand imagination
and not a single clue
as to how to make the last thought a reality.

CHANGES // FAMILIARITY

Lately I have not been doing things like I used to.
My writing has become different after so many years
of staying constant.
The motions of my fingers changing like the tides of the ocean
as the moon goes through its phases.

My thoughts do not rest,
a toddler running on a playground
from dawn till dusk.
The energy seemingly incomprehensible.

My left arm enters my shirt before my right,
my left leg enters my pants before my right—
I wonder if God is growing displeased with me.

The twitch in my fingers,
the shake of my hands,
as memories and emotions flood my mind.
My skull might have cracked
and blood might suffocate its very controller.

There is not a food that brings me delight.
My stomach does not feel flat,
but bloated.
As I wake,
as I work,
as I sleep.

My prayers go unfulfilled,
my voice goes unheard.
My mind becomes overwhelmed
from the what-ifs.

Change is good, they say.
Change is difficult, they say.
Change is needed, they say.

But what do I do
if I do not take well to change?

I KNOW MYSELF, BUT YOU SEEM TO KNOW MORE

I am ready to kill you,
a knife to your throat.
You smile at me in pure ecstasy,
and just mumble,
finally.

They say you do not truly know someone
until you do business with them,
travel with them, or live with them.
I have done all three with you for as long as
rain has showered Earth.

I have sat in cars with you,
traveling hundreds of miles daily.
I have made dealings with you,
which you have broken
and at times, honored. I have lived with you
every single day for the past couple of years.
You sleep with not a single inch
remaining between us.

I wonder what it will take
for you to leave me at peace,
and ending your life may
stop your whispers.

Smile with glee,
smile with glee—
I will let you go free
for the time being.

Please, just let me be.

ALL WHICH GOES WITH YOU

A lifeless body lay in my view,
wrapped in a pure white silk garment from head to toe.
A wooden box encasing them
for the rest of eternity.

A white silk garment—
that is all we take from this world into the grave.
Our deeds and misdeeds
sit on our shoulders,
anxiously waiting to present
their case for if we should attain
forever peace, or torture.

We are simple beings when we die.
We may live lavishly, or decently,
but we all go down the same way.

In the eyes of many,
our only currency is actions.
What we did in our lives
to help mankind, or hurt it.

CYCLES

There are nights
I tell myself that this is it.
I plan for everything,
and hope that an end is near.

There are tears,
there is frustration, there is anger.
There is every emotion
compiled into a person
who does not have the slightest idea
how to get rid of them.

My head aches—
the pounding of a hammer would be more soothing.
There is a distinct pain about mental adversities
that hurts deeply;
I cannot name a physical pain
that compares to it.

I plan, I commit,
and I cannot follow through.
The cycles must continue.

ZIKR

God forgives those who are remorseful,
God finds those who seek.

If that is enough to conjure your attention,
then why have I not done so already?

Throughout the many moons of the past months,
I have not given the time to properly give you my attention,
and for you to give me yours.

At the first tear drop of strife,
I am back in your arms,
and you cradle me so dearly,
like a mother with her newborn baby.
I am weak—
I am weak without your strength.

So why do I,
out of all the seconds in my measly days,
forget to cherish you in the best of times?

How selfish have I become to forget the one thing
that helps the most when all is well,
and remember it through the wrinkles in my fingers
when all is lost?

FLEETING CONTENTMENT

I fill my mind with goals,
believing that achieving them will reward me
by filling ounces of a ditch that hardships dug within me.
Or give me a small monument for my efforts,
one which would keep my gaze from the eyesore.

A temporary distraction
from what may always hurt me.

PERCHED SUNFLOWER CONVERTIBLE

There is a bright yellow car
that is perched on a building.
Off the highway, watching all of its own
come and go.

That car
which I stared at as a child,
wondering when the day would come
where I could hop in its cockpit
and drive off the ledge.
Freeing it from its captivity.

A drive down an autumn-laden highway,
leaves flurrying around the roofless car.
Hair mingling with the wind,
and gentle kisses from a sweet lover.

Autumn drove past many times.
My eyes would stop seeing that car I admired,
only able to remember it when I was on the highway,
wondering when I would come back to it.

And one day I came back to that car,
riddled with rust,
the building it stayed perched on
painted with graffiti.

Parts of me knew I had to come to terms,
that I was too late to liberate it.
And parts of me ached,
knowing the dream
which I had kept hidden from the world as a child
would never come to be.

VAST LANDS // LOST SOULS

Moments of youthfulness / constant prayers,
begging to have the life
I would always recognize.
No matter the land or oceans that came between,
no matter how much time had passed.

As that youth developed,
I walked off the foundation, which was built
by the bloodied hands of immigrants,
hoping to land in a place I could call my own.

Only to lose sight of the grips, which were made
for flocking chicks.
Falling toward the ground / floating with the clouds.
Feeling as if destiny were not in my own hands.

And with the distance, my eyes unfocused. Looking for home,
but becoming lost within the vast lands of this world.

18 'TIL I DIE

My mind and body
feel a lot heavier today.
My limbs have become weights,
and even moving them slightly
brings a feeling of achievement.

Rain shatters on the shingles,
glass plummeting from the sky above
so fiercely that one would think
those little droplets
were unmercifully chasing after a certain target.

The thunder shakes my core,
the quick flashes of lightning
give me glimpses of how powerful
nature can be;
yet the thought of a godless universe
prances around my mind,
ignoring everything that just occurred.

You tell me that smiling brings good fortune,
yet I cannot bring myself to crack my still mouth.
You say prayers are accepted no matter what,
yet I cannot seem to cusp my hands.
You say that there is a forgiving entity seated
above the seven layers of heaven,
yet I do not think I will ever be forgiven.

If living is beneficial,
let me live.
If dying is beneficial,
let me die.
Do whatever is best for me,
for I do not know myself.

The rest of the days are in your hands now.

PUSHING THORNS

For so many months,
I heard your voice
ring through my ears,
even though you were
nowhere near me.

For many years,
I have barreled down the stairs
and seen an eerily empty
living room.
The couches are firm,
and there is a single stick of incense
burning away on the table.

I have shed tears over home
not feeling like home—
my bed not feeling
like my body was molded for it.
Every time I enter through this door,
I have walked into a foreign country
and not known a soul in this land.

I would be a liar if I said
things have been better after the change.
I am not in between your spring-like tension,
but I feel as if I was thrust into
another mess that I was far from ready for.

I wonder if this mess has affected everyone
and not just me.
There have been many nights I desired
to drink my life away,
to self-medicate and feel utterly nothing.

By all means, there will be a sigh
of contentment once I see the sign to
this measly town in my rearview mirror
one final time.

OCEAN OF PRESSURES

I, a misfortunate soul trapped within a case
of despair.
One which is locked from the outside
and thrown in an ocean
that holds none of life's answers.
Bystanders peering on the outskirts,
seeing if I am the chosen one;
the one who escapes
before the air begins to turn against me.

And I, knowing that this case will crash
on the seabed at any moment—
knowing that my time is sprinting.
Knowing that if I would like to save myself,
I need a miracle.

A KNIFE, A COCONUT, AND A PALM

My mother's palm fresh with blood—
if there is a heaven on earth,

I've heard the door is beneath
a mother's sole.

Bang on it all you'd like—
it'll refuse to open

even for her child.
I lie there, fatigued.

That's when you'll know all of me.
Under bruised palms and

aching lungs.
Her blood drips onto the marble counter,

the knife on the floor, its tip rose-red, and I make sure
my tongue is there to greet it.

ANTI-ELEGY (AFTER MARCI CALABRALTA)

For my mother, who came here as a teenager
working twelve-hour days, not because we needed the money,
but because it was all she ever knew.

For my father, who learned English from
watching New York Jets football and listening to rap
on the radio. Knowing his mother back home
was on her deathbed. His father's grave in a lot which
he won't be buried in.

For my grandfather, who would tell my mother
to get whatever my palms landed on. That he did not
hop country after country only for her to not be giving.

For my sister, ravaged to her cement foundation,
who carries unceasing strength.
For my sister, one of the first women I've loved deeply.
For my sister, who hangs up missing posters of herself
on utility poles.

I am a barren land,
plant what you will.

THERE IS NO CHANGE

My body refuses you
at the front door. You stay

banging. Until the hinges come loose,
the wood splinters.

No one mentions the weight,
gravity burying knees into the ground,

heads not being raised,
how much past events truly pin you down.

And so the door always caves,
the swarm will always envelope those who run the farthest.

One thing is for certain:
your blood will always be in this body.

So I rise.

WEDDING DAZE

You held my hand before
the beat coursed through our bodies.

The crowd gathered,
I can't remember the last time

you touched my skin.
Rough palms which I've grown to hate.

They say with old age comes
childlike tendencies.

An extra light on to sleep.
Needing extra hands to stand.

On the day everyone was celebrating love,
I only thought of you.

Why your fingers interlocked mine when
they never had before.

How could I feel love from the same hands
that brought me pain.

How could I feel love from the one
who advocated for its nonexistence.

WITH AGE

Everything I do is for you.
How sugar drops from the edge of
the spoon / the way the car merges in between
others / the scars on my knees / the crinkle in my palms
when I speak to you.

Can you hear me?
When my memories are filled with bliss,
when I hold a knife to my wrists?
When I pray to you above,

do you know it's signed from me?

I was always taught to fear;
these days my family is attempting to learn

how to love.

FAULTY FOUNDATION

Lately, I have been feeling like a prisoner.
Have I truly walked through the swamp that is my past?
Or have I attempted to build on something
that was never meant to be covered up in the first place?

ONLY THEN

Maybe in another life
you would stare at me pleasantly,
like the moon does every night
and the sun does with dawn.

Your presence would be a calm breeze
filled with yellow and brown leaves.
A wind that only fall
and nostalgic memories could bring.

Your embrace would be like waves baptizing
parts of me I had no thought of existing.
Washing away all the anger and pain
I carried throughout life.

I can see it now—I can feel it now.
I cannot bring myself
to forgive you until then.

II – IQAMA

Let us stand together, as one. Let unity be our defining factor.

We would be told to stand together, feet aligned, shoulders touching. I always thought of it as our veins being connected, us being one entity rather than many different ones.
The same blood running through all of us, our thoughts intertwined like tree branches touching one another in a dense forest. Mind emptying and being filled with a euphoric feeling, right before we were about to begin.

POTENTIAL

Have you looked at the ground lately?
The way the grass grows, petals flourish,
and flowers rise?

Have you heard that the Prophet Adam
was made of dirt? Clay from the ground—
as we all are.

He was branded holy.
We are not and yet
he lived in the same body as us.

Perhaps this was a message.
A little bird told me that it is so.
To show that we were created
with the same materials
as those most holy.

SUPPORT

There is love in the conversations we share.
Whether we talk about my life
or your strengths,
we never grow tired of the endless words.

There have been times when I have lost faith in you,
and I am sure you have lost patience with me.
We go in circles,
'round and 'round repeatedly.

Our love is relentless.
You keep on calling me back,
and I staunchly ignore you.
Oh, how foolish of me!
I come crawling back to you anyway.

But you are not upset with me,
nor do you tell me that you told me so.
You accept me
and all of my flaws and mistakes.

Keep on trying, I believe in you.
Keep on going, I trust your growth.
Keep on loving, for I will never leave you.

We have each other,
and as long as that is certain,
I will not be as hopeless
as I once was.

A MEANING IS BETTER THAN NONE

I picture the beginning of me
being discussed over a cup of
sweetened, condensed-milk-filled chai.
How you'd poetically lace
your words in Urdu.

Maybe it's time to have a son.

I imagine, over and over again.

We have had two daughters.
I desire a son I can teach my experiences to.

And so, the chai finishes,
and you both do as well,
or only you do.
I am planted soulfully,
and while you write your own plans for me,
another has already destined my life
to unfold even before you can acknowledge
that I exist.
An entity derived from you,
but so drastically different from the way you imagined.

And the day I was born,
I was not only made from you,
but was stamped with a name
you had chosen.

The bringer of happiness and joy,
a meaning I grew distant from,
like a sinking ship separated from life
and decaying into the depths of the unknown.

The smiles you had lessened as time went on,
and it seems I mirrored those gestures as well.

The call to prayer being announced in my ears,
but not a single soul praying afterward.
I am anxiously idling by,
waiting for my prayer to begin.

It would have begun
if I hadn't hesitated handing my life
to the selfish, impulsive tendencies that reside in my body
like a vital organ.

And it seems ironic that one of the
more damaging persons in my life
could have given me a name with such
a pleasant meaning,

the bringer of happiness and joy.

UNHEALTHY SUBMISSIONS

My hands bound,
legs tied to the ground.
I am helpless, and my mind can have its way
with me, just as it pleases.

Show me your tortuous tendencies
or sporadic mercy.
I hope for the latter;
I hope for at least a speck of love this time.

I may very well attempt to escape,
but I have done as much as I can in the past,
and know most actions are futile.

There was a moment where the bindings loosened.
I found that out when I began to love and be happy for myself,
but they would tighten as soon
as I once again lost hope.

There is a flower sprouting within me, though.
One which refuses to wither,
as it knows that it will one day see the sun again
without a worry in the world.

ARCHEOLOGICAL DIGGING

I dig like a person
on a mission, desperate to find solutions
but failing to discover contentment.

ALL I DESIRED WAS YOUR HAPPINESS

A carpet littered with photo albums.
Children of the past staring above—
moments gone by in a blink of an eye,
time escaping quicker than one
can speak their vows.

In those photos, there is a blissful nostalgia.
A kind so rosy,
and one that stands still.
A terrible longing to go back
in time if it were humanly possible.

I wonder now
if you find slivers of peace
without my presence.

PARENTAL MISGUIDANCE

A bird who trips out of its nest,
its safe haven getting lost within the branches.
Hitting the ground, as light as a feather.
Left to fend for itself until help soon comes.

Parts of me
I have launched off skyscrapers
in the hopes of a bystander picking them up
or getting lost in the crowds,
and me never dealing with them again.
But I've felt a deep hurt in the aftermath,
a bruise to the very bone,
to the ego in wanting those parts again to complete me.

The ache of regret in knowing that there was a possibility
of me cleansing those parts of me
if I had given a little more effort in their care
instead of abandoning them
and making them nature's children.

DOG DAYS

Your idea of love is submission.
Acting on every word you say;
me kissing the ground you walk on
and putting your happiness over my own.
To feel comfortable with you hovering over me,
and to be content with the leash
you tied around my neck.

Instead of loving me out of the bond we share,
your love sways with how much control you hold.
And I will not lock myself in a kennel
for your love any longer.

I have lost out on so much of my youth,
and I will not waste more time on a love
with as many strings as yours.

FROZEN IN TIME

I am frozen in time,
suspended in air,
arms out as if I am reaching.
I do not fall,
I am not lifted.
I am the man frozen in time, after all.

Some exclaim that I am
stuck with the past,
like an archeological dig.
The churches of the ancient Greeks,
or the fossils of many beasts
that even we would be afraid of in this day.

The world is many moons old,
and I have not lived them all.
I have heard the stories of great floods
and seas parting,
illiterate men even becoming holy,
but I have not seen them with my own eyes.

Ephialtes betrayed his homeland
for a sort of Persian reward.
How strong must loyalty have been in that era
to lose it over a piece of gold or two.

Alexander never succumbed to
the fate of a warrior,
and yet died when at his greatest height.
Some say poison, some say illness.
No one but God knows the answer to our debates.

I am frozen in time.
I do not fall,
nor rise.
The past leaks onto me
like ink dripping onto paper,
and the present desperately clings onto me,
holding me dearly so I do not drown
in the depths of all that has not been discovered.

GROUND ZERO

There are moments of unsteadiness,
where the ground in my mind is unleveled.
The green liquid encasing the air bubble
moving back and forth.
A pendulum swinging left to right.
Right to left.

The air grows stale,
dust from falling buildings
and leaves from branches breaking.
I take deep breaths,
air traveling down into my lungs
to the very depths of my own weak structure.

In this madness I do not find meaning,
but illogical thoughts—
a panic-inducing daze.
One which sends my thoughts fleeing,
searching for sanctuary in areas that
will only hurt them more.

I cough, wheeze, hold my throat.
Begging to breathe fresh air by the sea
as my feet sink into golden sand.
Walking,
dust billowing from my lungs,
knowing all in me is ground zero.

Knowing that this restructure will take its sweet, sweet time.
Knowing that I must build myself more secure
so I do not repeatedly collapse again and again.

BALLADS OF PRIDE

I search between the olive branches,
wondering if I will come across you again.
That is where I left you years ago—
in a brown woven basket
on a warm spring day
at the very roots of the tree.

There is rain being birthed from above;
the branches do not provide safety any longer.
I am a fool to believe that you would have stayed
in that basket after all these years.

I dream about your travels.
To all you have seen—where you could have possibly gone,
and all that you have made without me.
I wonder if you are content—
or have you found another
to fill the void I left?

It was an ill-advised divide,
one which I believed would benefit the both of us.
Yet here I am,
searching for you again.

Not knowing if you are in
the same predicament as me.

PEACE, IN DUE TIME

Even though you are far gone,
I still carry an ache—
the itch to feel your warmth.
To know how sanctuary in oneself
may feel again.

And I acknowledge that
in some moments my progress is slow,
but like two lovers who are written to meet
in a lifetime,
I know that I will make my way back to you.

WHO WILL WE BECOME?

I read endless stories
of loved ones returning
after many years apart.

So long after that they do not
recognize each wrinkle
or gray hair that appears.

And they are filled with regret
at the fact that they missed
the opportunity of memories being created.

A once-in-a-lifetime event
which you can only hear about,
but never witness for yourself.

I have read endless stories
of humans dying with anger in their hearts.

And I do not know

what the future holds for us.

GROWING DILEMMAS

I am fighting between you
and all that is good for me—
for a reason I do not know myself.
Perhaps the acceptance you could give
would let me die happily,
or maybe you could grant me
heavenly wishes I could not
achieve otherwise.

But on the other side
there is a concrete good.
And not being suspended without an answer.
So, I question why
I torture myself between the two,

one filled with inconsistency
and the other only having proof.

I'M ENDING TODAY

How a single life is a generation. A history book. How all of humanity rests between my limbs and courses through me. I am merely root, and yet I forget how to water myself. A plant cannot live if you do not love it. How can I stand to love myself when I've grown to hate the eyes looking back at me? How can I truly love humanity, the generations to come, when the dirt beneath me is already rotten?

I would rather not let them break the soil. I would rather not fill the world with more melancholy.

AFTERSUN

Sweat builds out of my pores.
Moonlight shines through the crack in the blinds.
There is no other voice left in this world.

Tonight, it is only me

and the hum of the car. A deep, unsatisfying
dull roar that can die out any second.

I sink into the sand,
my hands grasping only that which will leave them.

The sea breathes my name.
Water has already greeted me.

For once, I would like your arms to wrap around me

as I attempt to begin again.

REVOLUTION

You may eviscerate my body—
I'll gladly let the only commodity left of
me be the poems I've written.

MALE. AGE 20. APRIL, 2016

A cloudless night,
fluorescent lights mobbed with bugs—
the train's holler getting louder.
Not a soul here but God and I.

Momma, I have never spoken
of the urge to leap.

SAIL

A finger pressed to my temple,
blue eyes pierce me.

At times, I wander into oceans,
I become a current

without purpose. Very rarely have
I acknowledged my own existence.

Am I truly real? I pinch my skin.
My arms are weary from fighting back.

Historians do not research
the battles in one's mind.

Many dead soldiers lay here,
their bodies stacked upon one another,

overflowing.
I could tell you each of their stories if you'd like.

I'll tell you what the angels see
when I get there.

Won't you listen?

TWO EVILS

I wish I could have saved her,
gripping her wrist so tightly

that she would think I am
the lesser of two evils. Imagine

your own blood being afraid of
you. The fruits that have grown on

branches want nothing more than
to fall. The words they speak

replicate bullets. The punches
thrown become dormant, waiting

for an explosion to take place. I
have been told the most love

is shown after skin ripples.
Guilty conscience speaking

but refusing to see itself
in the mirror. And so I look at you,

you plead this time is different.
Years have stacked on one another.

You grab my mouth,
pouring all you hoard into me,

and

my grip loosens.

HOLLOWED-OUT BOY

You knock on my skin,
asking if there is still life in there.
Your knuckles pull away before the echoes
crash against the mark you've left.

ALONE ON MY WEDDING DAY

My back aches—the mattress isn't here yet.
It's been a month.

Every Monday morning I am woken up
by the moans of lawn mowers. I think back

to my teenage years as if they are
merely fever dreams.

My mother started loving me the day after I left.
How do I tell her it's too late?

That she dug me in so deep
that I am beyond suffocating.

My father—I won't waste any more words for you.
I know you and I are facing different directions.

Here I am, inches from my wedding day.
All whom I'm supposed to love

too far to reach. There are no lights hung up, no one is smiling.
Silence fills the wordless conversations.

Perhaps it's been my fault all along.

WAKING UP NEXT TO DEMONS

A tug on my shoulder as I wake, a
gentle, tender kiss—
so loving that it makes me want
to crawl back under, back into your arms.

The heat of hell screams
from between your ribs,
echoing off my body—
the warmth that I have been longing for,
the warmth I have been told
that I should call home.

With acceptance,
I melt into your arms. Snow on skin,
becoming one with the many
you have already taken.

My body feeble and mind numb.
Perhaps I will try
to get slip out of bed at the coming of dawn.

III - SALAAH

You look at me as if I am one whom you love,
even after all that I have done. Why?

And when we began, we became equals in the eyes of the beholder. We were all doing one thing, participating in the greatness of God, and thinking of every inch of this beloved universe. I was taught the motions as a child. When to rise and to fall. What to say when my body would bend over in *Ruku.* How to pray, ingrained on my newborn slate. No matter how far I stray, it'll be the one thing I will never forget.

YOUR WORDS COULD FEED

You sparsely speak as the hours pass.
I tend to wonder if now you have grown mute
or taken an oath of silence.

The doors are closed,
lights off from dusk till dawn,
and the silence speaks volumes
through the cracks in the walls,
the creases in the floorboards,
underneath the crevices of the doors.
Loud enough that I find myself
covering my ears
and begging the terrible noise to stop.

A memory of my parents fighting,
us hiding wherever we could find solace.
Beneath blankets where our soundproof ignorance lay.

I find myself distressed.
In fetal position
leaning on my bed frame.
Tears steamrolling down my hot face,
trailblazing paths that others will soon take.

The silence does not stop.
You do not speak.
I have thought, if you loved me,
you would tell me to my face—
not by a stocked fridge
or paying the bills.
You would not make me walk through this maze,
trying to find out if you do what you do
out of care
or because you birthed me.

As grateful as I am for all that you do,
I would gladly starve
if it meant I would not have to long
for your voice.

FALLING INTO YOU

You are derived from flowers
and trees / nature's own beauty.
Begging you to come home.

You are the sweet nectar
that spills from a soft mango,
dripping with even the slightest touch
of my knife.

You are the color when the sun wakes
and when the moon dreams,
rustling in its slumber.

The rain that drips from above,
the snow that blankets the earth.
All reminders that all must touch
the ground once more.

All reminders that my love for you
is eternal.
As far as the eye can see,
as wide as this land stretches.

A reminder that I am yours
I am yours
I am yours

And there may be nothing in this world
that will be able to change that.

HINDSIGHT

Many moments have passed,
ones where I could have done good,
but did nothing instead.
We live and learn constantly—
for when those moments come again
I will be the first to jump
and take the chance at doing something worthwhile.

OWN BONDS

My forehead still reaches the prayer mat,
my fingers still touch the ground with glee.
My whispers are only heard by God,
my heart can only plea.

My practice is for God and me alone—
onlookers can comment as they please.

BELIEF

I wish to see
your magnificence even in
the prayers left unanswered.

TRUDGING THROUGH THE STORMS

While I have not been myself as of late,
there is a vague memory of how I once used to
cherish the moments I had.
A memory that propels me from disparity
to a wistful thinking—
that boy who used to smile for no reason,
one who would laugh with every ounce of air
that would touch his lungs,
a being who felt present in time,
and not one who was spectating
life as if it were a movie.

And an immense yearning
to reach that memory—
not wanting my knees to give out
until I do.

RUNNING TO SELF-CONTENTMENT

I have been running
from start to finish
out the door
and eventually back through
in a handful of pieces.

From gravel, which flew with every step,
to soft dirt roads molding to the shape
of your own foot.
To cement.

For so long, my feet moved one after another.
Only for my knees to squeak,
and eventually cave in on their own home.

For so long I have been running,
attempting to find home
in what may bring me contentment.
Time and time again I have been faltering,
wondering why peace does not enter my abode.

Perhaps I need to quit running to what calls my name.
I need to take a seat and examine how I can become
comfortable in what already lies
in my own body.

THE BATTLE FOR FREEDOM

There are small moments
when I put all my strength against
the floor I am on.
To push myself up,
to stand tall against that
which knocked me down.

Bruised, battered, and broken,
my legs pick me up
with the knowledge that it
may very well be my last stand.
The kind historians will write melodies after,
the kind loved ones
will remember fondly.

I struggle until there's no longer a struggle left.
I stand until I do not need to anymore.
I fight until my voice cannot raise again.

And the cycle continues—
my will siding with a hope of victory.

SOMBER

I scream with the radio / let their cries become mine / among the misfits and angels / I drive / through roads / barriers / the gates of hell reaching out and scarring my flesh / the way she says my name brings tears to my eyes /

if purpose was a person / it would be you.

WE LEARN AS WE LIVE

There is a feeling,
intense—as if gravity dissipates from thin air.
My heart moving slowly up
from the bottom of my throat.

This world does not teach you
how to combat implosions.
Each and every beam holding your body upright
suddenly not being able to do what they have always done.

And so we learn on our own,
the gravities, inconsistencies,
the way we are supposed to heal the cracks.

All the many wonders of this earth.

MARCH 2023

A *Jummah* in Japan is where I prayed earnestly for the first time since I was nineteen. The warmth of the water still resides in my face, the residue still stuck to my fingers. I recall, vividly, the sensation of vomiting. Either from the Lawson's egg salad sandwich I quickly ate beforehand or the devils leaving my body—possibly even both. (Bourdain might roll in his grave for the first part, my father for the latter.) Again, I felt like a child in both ways, in prayer and in action. Again, I felt unreal.

I became whole.

IGNITION

I am not told there is nature
blooming between my joints,
or that the blood that rushes through
my veins is like heaven's rivers—
sweet like honey, and tranquil
to the very touch.

You force me to believe
I am what I am not.
And though I know what I am not,
the tired child in me who still worships your feet listens
and sows your words into me with
their tiny, fumbling fingers.
Still, after all these years, believing your words to be gospel.

And you wait for those wretched flowers to blossom,
so the world can see exactly where your mind
wanders when you catch a glimpse of me.

I will burn this field before I give you
the pleasure of watching those stems escape the dirt.

FOR YOU, FOR ME

Spilled sugar resting on granite
for the spring ants to feast /
weepings / sorrowful mo(u)rnings
where we reminisce what was and what will be.

A benign root sown,
your lips like sugar on the tip
of my newborn tongue. If only rewinding was as quick
as watching TV, I would do so before a heart could beat.

Beat the fire alarms as they blare,
ethnic cookings burning
with a God-sent smell of home away from home,
where the people would only frown at our imitations.

Two tablespoons of sugar,
which drip out the sides of the spoon,
a wallop of milk.
The fragrance lingering from the night before,
making its way into the tea.

You sit there calmly;

I wonder where our next conversation will lead.

DEVASTATION–

My father telling me I couldn't buy chips
from the corner store after prayer.

Failing tests, losing races. Numb to the circled number on pages,
numb to the blood-red numbers buzzing at the finish line.

My hands on my waist as I walked from room to room.
My father saying I was the reason he was leaving,
my mother's mouth still, as if she had become a statue. A statue.

The stars were beautiful, I thought.
OxyContin in my palms,
I took a step off the platform.

Devastation—
A cigarette butt crushed under your foot,
cupping my earlobe with your tongue,
telling me I'm not the one for you.

Bruises on my sister's face,
punches thrown where she could not see.

My neck, gripped.
Not even a breath allowed to escape.

If my life was not this

I wonder if I would have lived at all.

IV – SALAAM

May peace be upon you.

By the end, our heads turn to the angels resting on our shoulders. But not only our shoulders, also the person next to us. Sending them peace and blessings as our faces meet theirs for that very second. Being one that helped build a bridge of peace in another.

THE WIND AND THE WEEDS

The soft meadow is nudged gently
by a wind known fondly to it.
The wild grass may ask,

Oh, you again. What brings you to the meadow once more?

and the wind touches the blades and says,

I desired to visit old friends.

The wind comes and goes,
cherishing the meadow only he knows.
Even as the seasons change,
he visits all that is familiar to him.
Until one day he comes no more,
while the meadow is left to believe
the wind has found one worth more.

THE SIMILARITIES WE SHARE

Have you ever thought about the moon?
How it is still there
despite it disappearing
on some nights?

Have you ever thought about the stars?
Glistening light-years away—
more so than we will ever live.
The same stars
generations before gazed upon,
and our future will as well.

And our sun,
shining valiantly for us
and then for someone else
who we may never meet.
Surely, the only quality
I will ever know about them
is that they shared
the same view as me.

Have you ever thought about
how two humans meet?

Despite the many people this world holds,
my and your stories collided,
creating a larger star, light-years away
which all may see.

RISING FROM THE ASHES

One after the other,
I am abandoned,
reminiscing about the same movements
my father exhibited when
he wanted to start anew.

The human body is made up
of skin and bones,
blood gushing through veins
repeatedly, a job done nearly sixty times a minute.
And yet we are more than just that.

I am a shell of my former self;
my passion has dwindled,
and so has my own will to live.
I am not the same person who fell in love with this life,
innocently calling it mine.

My personality flees at the danger I convince myself
that I am in.
Hopping on trains and planes,
cars and even bikes.
They flee and do not intend to return.

I am hollow,
a relic of a previous version.
And while emotions are difficult to come by,
I only hope they come back to their motherland,
knowing that it is safe once again.

AND SO IT GOES

These decisions are difficult,
but they are needed
if you aspire to grow
out of the shell
you have limited yourself to.

With everything laid before your eyes,
do not be afraid to take steps forward.
This is the land of opportunity;
it has been penned as such.

The past may call,
at times desperately,
but that is the test
you will be given.
You may grow
or succumb.

In order to scaffold accordingly,
you must build properly.
There must be a foundation
if you want to move forward.
If the beginning is weak,
you will not learn the next step.

Do not feel sorry—
the past is the past,
and it will not vanish.
It will be buried under new memories
if only you allow it such opportunity.

And so it goes.

GROWTH TOWARD THE SUN

The scars on my skin remind me of moments
that tie me down.
To a point where I overthink all that
I could have done different.
Knowing that I never have another opportunity to redo days of old.

But like a plant after winter, I will always grow again.
Despite the way the plant tossed and turned in the garden,
it will be given another opportunity
to come out on the straight path it was
destined to trace all along.

WHAT THE ROADS HOLD

Along the journey
I have greeted many souls,
some too good for a sinner like myself
and others too wicked—
I did not desire the meat on my bones
to grow any more tainted.

And then there are some who warm
my heart at the very first impression.
Even though they may not wholly be like myself,
they resemble a warmth deep within them,
one that feels natural to be around.

Perhaps this is what it feels like to be accepted.

TAKING ADVANTAGE

The peace within my chest—
cool water encasing my heart,
running through my veins
as if it were always there
and I just had not paid any attention to it.

This feeling,
oh, how much I want it to last,
but knowing that if it
were always there,
I would not acknowledge it like I do now.

STANDING UP FOR PAST LIVES

I have dehumanized myself
for the sake of others' comfort.
Making a mockery of my own God-gifted vessel.
Over the width of my ears,
cracks in my teeth,
and squint in my eyes.

I have made jokes of how
my name rolls off their tongue.
I would cower with fear in my seat
just to appease whoever stood in front of me.

I would let others despise my identity,
giving them permission to carry hatred
for a trait I had no power in changing.
I would allow them to call me names
that they would dare not say
to a soul who held more power than them.

My voice—
silent as a cricket once one
came too close.
Not because it did not affect me,
but because I was so frightened
that there was a possibility
my situation could grow worse.

Those trials might have not been survivable.

But all of this, the past
carries lessons one cannot see
while they transpire.
These memories call me
and tell me that certain events were crossing boundaries.
I should have stood on the line,
and not brushed off nor cared about them.
They were events I should have stood tall for.
For me
and all others.

And I can shout this into existence,
with all the certainty my body can hold:

history will not repeat itself.

WE ALL GOT OUR OWN PEOPLE

The love you carry is unmatched—
one which others envy,
one which only I get to have.

And I question how I have become so lucky,
only for God to tell me that I have not.
That she was made for me,
as I was for her.
As others are made for each other,
and they will one day find their companion
as I did.

As she was made for me—
as I was for her.
Sculpted. Destined for one another.
In stone, I suppose.
That no matter the distance
that was between us,
we would be by each other
once time became our ally.

ROOM FOR IMPROVEMENTS

There are gardens in you
which speak to me.
Wrapping their stems around my ankles,
sharing their growth—their sustenance.
The water draining down my pores,
the dirt tenderly caressing my skin.
The sun kissing the hair that flows down my forehead.

In your gardens, your flowers do not wither
in my presence,
but accept and open a path for me
to come and go as I please.

I AM YOURS, AFTER ALL

The night is young,
dark blue skies, white speckled stars,
and blankets of clouds covering them.

I wonder of those who I have loved.
If smiles still crack their lips,
if happiness for them fits.

I wonder of those who I have briefly met,
what struggles they have felt,
of the many stories they can tell.

I think of her,
the one who could not see life.
Whose pain could turn mountains to dust.

I reflect. I am
unknown to myself.
Questioning all that occurs.

And I ponder you,
The all-knowing, the author of the world.

If you show me anything worth going on for,
despite how small,

I will devote my warmth only to you.

IN L.A. WE WONDER

I sit on the balcony, continental coffee keeping me company.
My head is ringing as if someone brought a hammer to it—
unmercifully, with no regard for my future nor a thought of my past.
I am just another number.

I look around, smog covers the sun, the skyline is barely visible
despite the strain in my eyes. Dull sunlight rests on white buildings
and a crow's cries can be heard through the hundreds of mufflers
on the street.

I sip some of the bitter coffee, and wonder—
life is fascinating, is it not?

SELF-EXPLORATION

The reason I write is to find locked parts of myself—
to open a door I had not known existed.

TO WHO WE BURIED, TO WHO WE LEFT BEHIND

I talked to a friend,
who I reconnected with after two years, who told me

you can't grow in a place like that.

And while I agreed, I couldn't help but revisit past versions of myself who did end up blooming in a barren town. Whose parents fought constantly, who every aunty at the masjid called a bad influence, and who didn't belong with the majority at school.

To say I didn't grow would diminish my struggle.

After all, I grew enough will—one day—to have left.

about the author

F.S. Yousaf is a writer and educator from New Jersey. He has published four books of poetry: *Euphoria*, *Sincerely*, *Serenity*, and *Oaths*. He began writing in 2013 and has his BA in History and Secondary Education. He lives with his wife, Yusra, and their two cats, Stormi and Yuki.

You can follow him on Instagram at @fs.yousaf.